D1585096

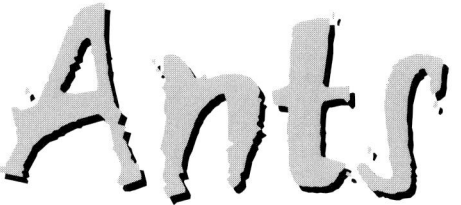

Ants

By Christy Steele

Raintree

www.raintreepublishers.co.uk
Visit our website to find out more information about Raintree books.

To order:
☎ Phone 44 (0) 1865 888112
▤ Send a fax to 44 (0) 1865 314091
💻 Visit the Raintree Bookshop at www.raintreepublishers.co.uk to browse our catalogue and order online.

First published in Great Britain by Raintree Publishers, Halley Court, Jordan Hill, Oxford, OX2 8EJ, part of Harcourt Education.
Raintree is a registered trademark of Harcourt Education Ltd.

Originated by Dot Gradations
Printed and bound in China by South China Printing

ISBN 1 844 21126 6
07 06 05 04 03
10 9 8 7 6 5 4 3 2 1

British Library Cataloguing in Publication Data
Steele, Christy
1. Ants – Juvenile literature
2. Rainforest ecology – Juvenile literature
595.7'96
A catalogue for this book is available from the British Library.

Acknowledgements
The publishers would like to thank the following for permission to reproduce photographs:
NHPA, pp. **7, 13**. USDA-ARS, pp. **4–5, 11, 20, 25** (left and right). Visuals Unlimited/ D. Cavagnaro, p. **1**; Milton Tierney, p. **8**; Nancy Wells, p. **12**; Brian Rogers, p. **14**; Walt Anderson, p. **16**; Glenn M. Oliver, p. **18**; David Ellis, p. **22**; Don Fawcett, p. **26**; George Loun, p. **29**

Cover photograph reproduced with permission of Corbis/Kevin Schafer

Every effort has been made to contact copyright holders of any material reproduced in this book. Any omissions will be rectified in subsequent printings if notice is given to the publishers.

Contents

Any words appearing in the text in bold, **like this**, are explained in the Glossary.

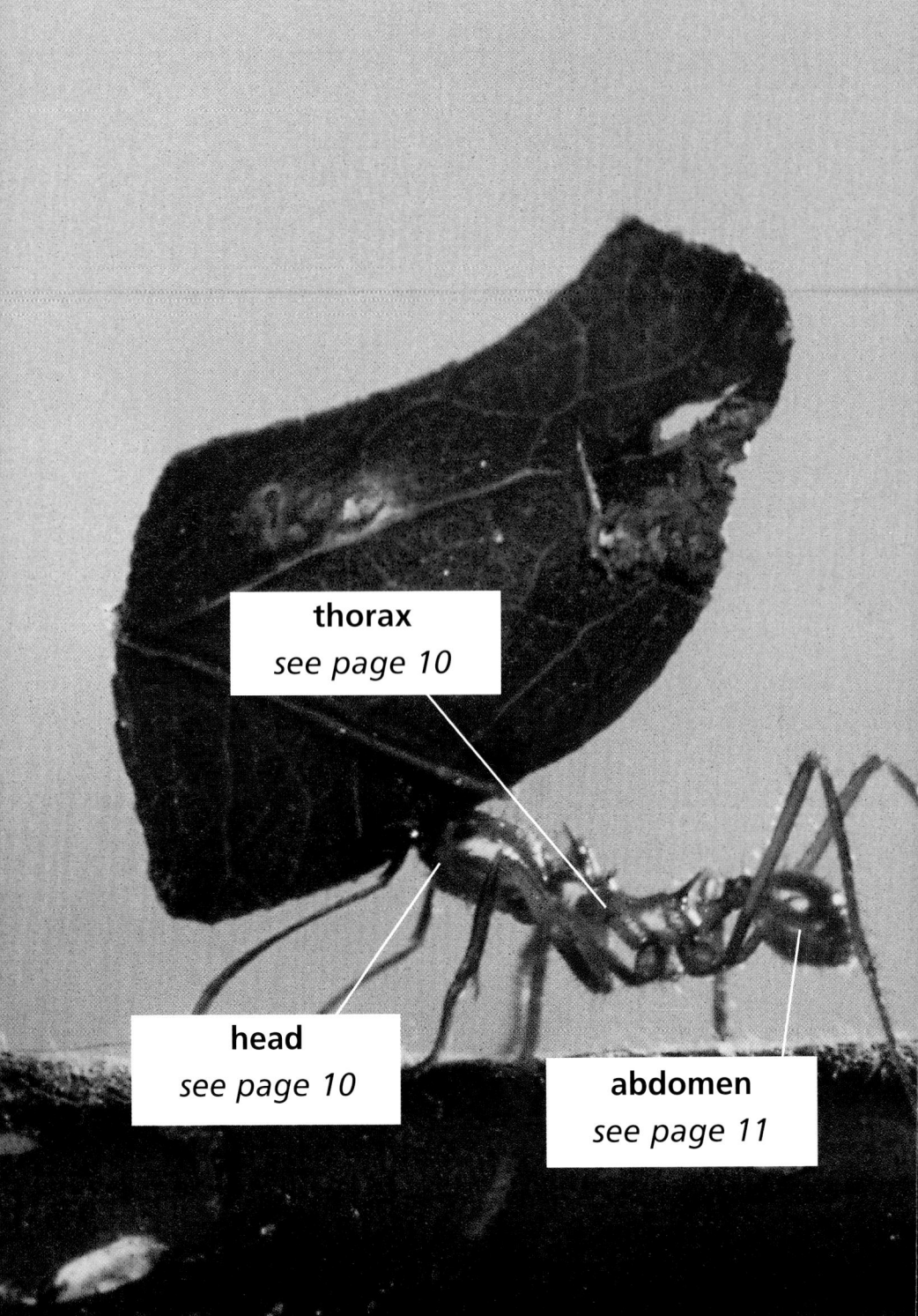

thorax
see page 10

head
see page 10

abdomen
see page 11

six legs
see pages 7, 10

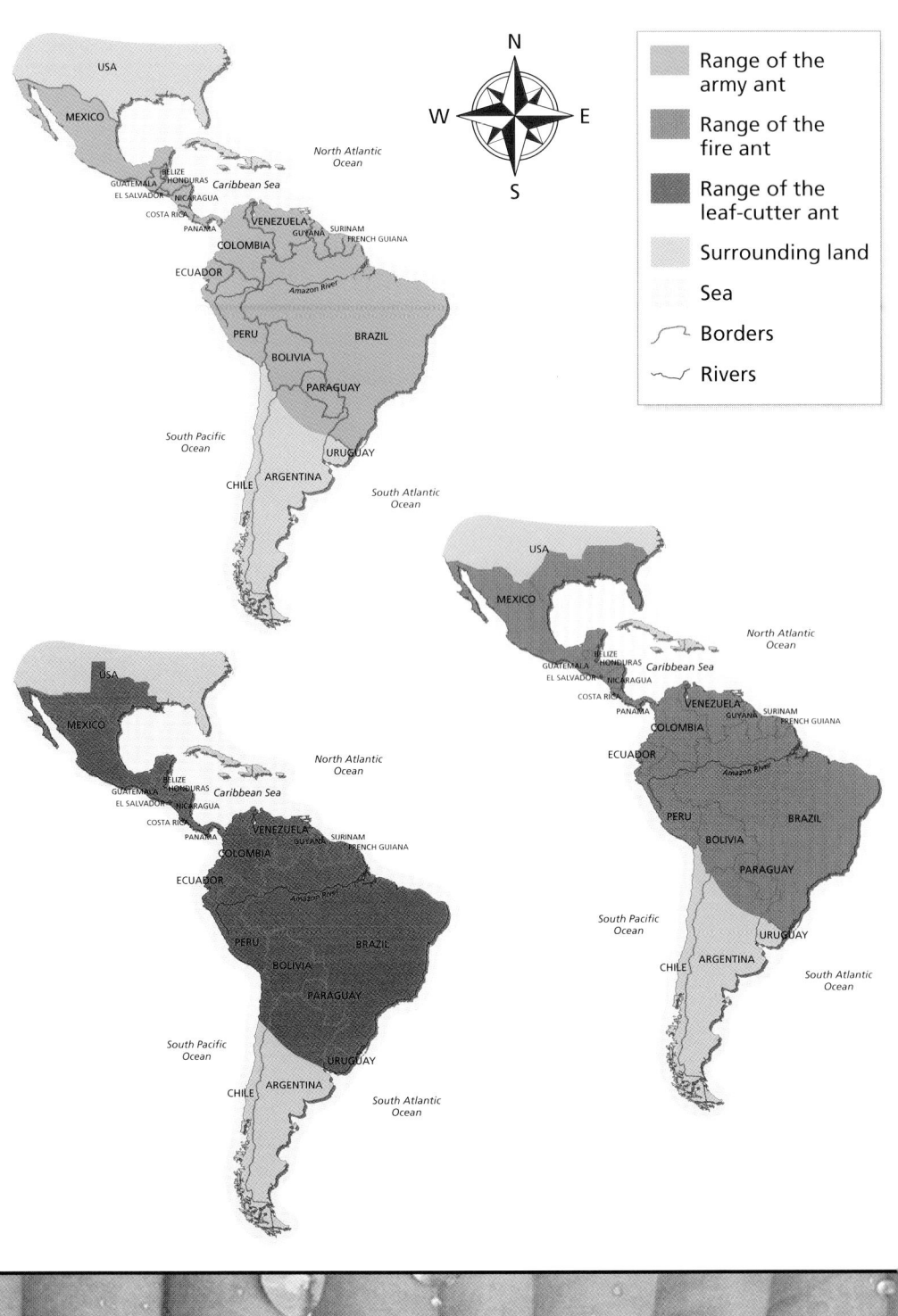

	Range of the army ant
	Range of the fire ant
	Range of the leaf-cutter ant
	Surrounding land
	Sea
	Borders
	Rivers

A quick look at ants

What do ants look like?
Ants are insects. They have three main body sections, six legs and two **antennae**.

Where do ants live?
The ants featured in this book live on the ground or in underground nests in and around rainforests.

What do ants eat?
Leaf-cutter ants eat a special kind of **fungus**. Army ants eat meat. Fire ants eat meat, seeds and nectar. Nectar is a sweet liquid found in flowers.

Do ants have any enemies?
Armadillos, anteaters, spiders, birds and many other animals and insects eat ants.

These leaf-cutter ants are bringing new leaf pieces to their nest.

Ants in the rainforest

There are thousands of known kinds of ants in the world. Most of these ants live in warm rainforests. Scientists believe that rainforests are home to many more kinds of ants that they have not even found yet.

Ants are an important part of the life cycle of the rainforest. They eat rainforest plants, other insects and nectar. Nectar is a sweet liquid found in flowers. But ants are also food for other animals. Armadillos, anteaters and many other animals eat ants.

This book is about army ants, fire ants and leaf-cutter ants. These kinds of ants live in many places in South and Central America. Many ants live in **Amazonia**. This is the largest rainforest in the world. It grows around the river Amazon.

Appearance

All ants have things in common. Ants have six legs. They all have bodies with three main sections. The first section of an ant's body is the head. The heads of different kinds of ants are different sizes and shapes.

All ants' heads have parts that help the ants sense the world around them. Antennae are feelers that grow on the top of ants' heads. Ants use antennae to touch, smell and taste. Most ants have eyes, but many are blind or cannot see well.

Ants have powerful outer jaws called **mandibles**. Mandibles move differently to people's jaws. They move from side to side like scissors, instead of up and down. Ants use mandibles to fight, to dig nests, to bite and to carry things, such as their food or their young.

The **thorax** is the middle part of an ant's body. An ant's six legs are attached to the thorax.

Fire ants have a thorax that is thinner than their head.

The back section of an ant's body is its **abdomen.** It contains two stomachs. Ants use one stomach to break down food they swallow. They use the other stomach to store some of their food. They bring food from this second stomach back up into their mouths to feed other ants. Some kinds of ants have stings on the end of their abdomens.

Some worker ants are in charge of digging and repairing the colony's nest.

Life in the colony

Ants are social insects. This means they live and work together in groups called **colonies**. Each ant has a special job to do.

The queen is a female ant that heads the colony. The queen's only job is to mate and lay eggs. All the other ants in the colony take care of the queen.

Drones are the only male ants in a colony. Their one job is to mate with a queen. Drones die when they have mated.

Ants give off special scents to send messages to other ants. They pass the scents by licking other ants or releasing the scents into the air. Ants may release scents that tell other ants they are in danger. Other scents lead ants to food. Scents help members of a colony to recognise each other. Soldier ants smell each ant trying to enter the colony. They will fight an ant that does not carry the colony's special scent.

Some kinds of ants have soldier ants that guard and protect the colony. Soldiers are bigger than the other ants. They often have larger mandibles to fight enemies. Enemy ants sometimes try to steal the colony's food. Other kinds of ants may take ants they catch back to their own colony to work.

Worker ants do many jobs in the colony. They feed the queen. They take care of eggs and larvae. Larvae are newly hatched ants. Nurse ants lick the eggs and larvae to keep them clean. Other worker ants clean the nest by removing waste. Some workers build a nest for the ant colony. Other workers look for food. These workers are called scouts or foragers.

Ants can carry objects that are up to 50 times their body weight. This worker ant will probably live for several months.

Life cycle

All types of ant have the same life cycle. They go through three stages of growth.

It usually takes ants about 30 days to grow from egg to larva to pupa to adult. The eggs, larvae and pupae of a colony are called its **brood**.

An ant spends the first part of its life in an egg. After a while, the egg hatches. Each kind of ant egg hatches at a different time.

Young larvae come out of the eggs. Larvae are small and worm-like. Worker ants feed and clean the larvae. Larvae eat and grow. They usually stay at this stage for a few weeks.

To enter the pupa stage, larvae spin cocoons around themselves. Inside these silky coverings, the larvae turn into pupae that look like fully formed adult ants. When the pupae are fully developed, they break out of their cocoons. They are then adult ants.

All ants work in the colony. Young adult ants begin life by becoming nurses. They take care of the growing brood. After a while, they begin other kinds of work. The oldest ants in the colony are the scout ants that look for food.

Most worker ants live for several months. Drones live for about one month. Queens live for up to eight years or more.

People often leave their villages when a column of army ants arrives. They come back after the ants have eaten all the insects and travelled to a new place.

Army ants

There are about 150 types of army ant. They are strong, meat-eating ants. They eat mostly insects. But they will also eat any other animal they can kill. They have strong jaws and can grow up to 2.5 centimetres long.

Army ants form long, wide lines as they move. A column of army ants can be more than 0.75 kilometres (0.5 miles) long. The way these ants travel looks like soldiers marching in an army. This is why people called them army ants.

Army ants live in huge colonies of up to 1 million ants. A large colony of army ants can eat up to 100,000 insects a day. They eat all the insects in one area quickly. The colony is always moving to look for more food.

Army ants may travel up to 350 metres from their nest to look for food.

Army ant nests

Army ants do not build permanent nests because they are always moving. Every night, they build a bivouac. The bivouac is a long, living chain of ants. Each ant hooks its mandibles and the claws on its legs on to another ant in the colony. The chain of ants wraps itself around the queen and the younger ants. In the morning, the ants unhook themselves and start moving again.

Army ants stay in one place for several days when larvae are spinning their cocoons to turn into pupae. At this time, the queen lays new eggs in the centre of the bivouac. The colony begins moving again only when the eggs hatch into larvae.

Hunting

Army ants use scents to find food. All the workers are blind. A scout leads a column of ants to look for food. They move forwards by following the scout's scent trails.

Army ants hunt in two ways. Sometimes the ants walk forwards in a thick column. Small groups of ants move out in different directions from the main column. From above, this looks like a tree. At other times, a huge group of ants makes a fan-like shape and sweeps forwards through the rainforest.

Once they have found food, lots of army ants crawl over the animal or insect. Their strong jaws bite small pieces off the animal. A group of army ants can turn an animal into a pile of bones in just a few hours.

People called these ants fire ants because their stings burn like fire.

Fire ants

There are many different kinds of fire ants. Each kind lives in its own special habitat. A habitat is where an animal naturally lives and grows. Fire ants can live on grasslands, flood plains or in lightly forested places in Amazonia.

Fire ants are small. They grow up to 6 millimetres long. Their colour ranges from red-brown to black. Some people fear fire ants because of their painful stings.

Unlike army ants, fire ants build underground nests that last a long time. Their nests are about 30 to 60 centimetres wide and several metres deep. The ants dig large, room-like areas called chambers. They dig tunnels to connect the chambers. A pile of loose soil is left on top of the nest after the ants have finished digging.

Fire ants are scavengers too. They will eat animals that they did not kill, such as this bird.

Hunting and eating

Fire ants eat other insects as well as plants and animals. They eat other ants. They also eat grains and seeds. Large groups of fire ants can destroy a farmer's crop by eating the seeds.

A fire ant scout hunts for any kind of food it can find. Sometimes it finds food that is too large for it to carry back to the nest. Then it leaves a scent trail to lead other workers to the **prey**. Prey are the animals and insects that fire ants eat.

Fire ants catch prey by stinging. First, they grab their prey with their mandibles. Then the fire ants use the sting on their abdomens to sting the prey. Each sting puts **venom** into the prey's body. The venom is a poison that slows down insects and animals. This makes the animals unable to run away from the ants.

The sting of one fire ant would not be enough to hurt most animals. So lots of ants get together to sting the animals. The combined venom of thousands of fire ants can slow down even large animals, such as young deer. Even so, most healthy animals can still escape from fire ants. Young or sick animals are in the most danger.

Fire ants then eat the animals they catch. They drink the juice and blood from their prey. In just one day, a group of fire ants can eat all of an animal except its bones.

Colony wars

Every fire-ant colony has its own nest. Fire ants rush out of the nest and sting anything that comes too close to it.

Each colony also has its own territory. A territory is a space the ants know well. The ants live and hunt in the colony's territory. Fire ants will fight to protect their territory.

A fire-ant colony will sometimes fight another one for more territory. This happens when many fire-ant colonies live close together in a small space. There may not be enough food for all the fire-ant colonies. Sometimes workers attack another colony's territory to find food. This starts a fight between the colonies.

Fire-ant colonies are small when they are first formed. Sometimes many new, small fire-ant colonies are close together. One of the new colonies may try to grow larger by stealing broods from other colonies. This causes a fight. Workers in the winning colony will enter the losing colony's nest and take away the brood. When the ants hatch, they become workers for the winning colony.

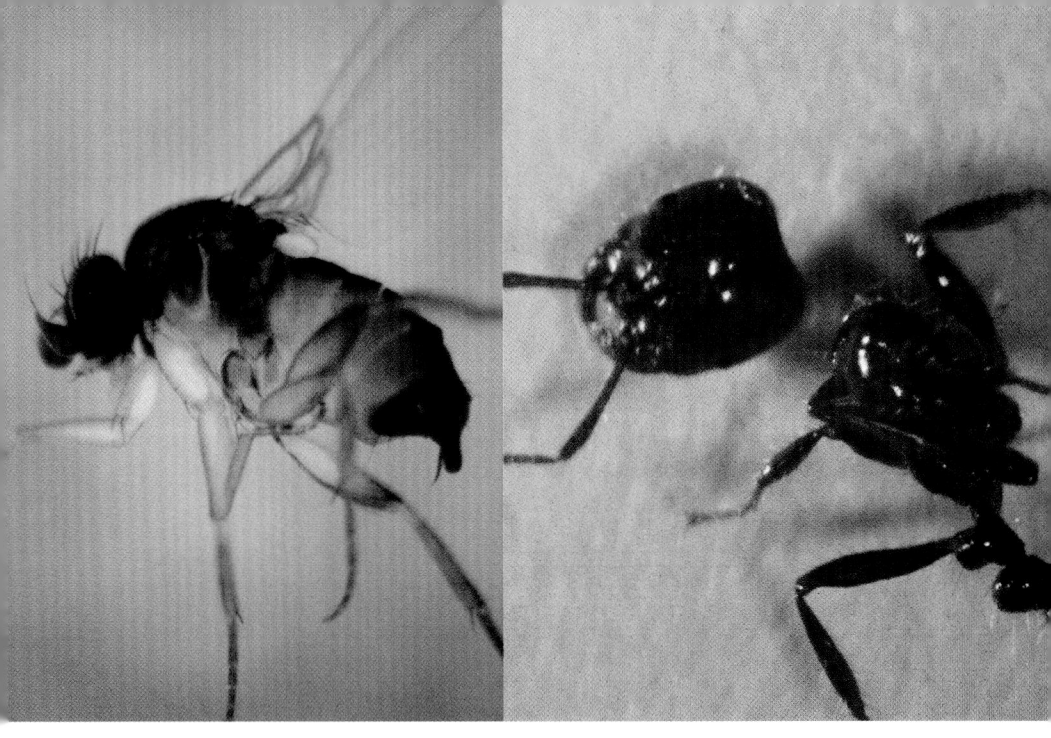

A phorid fly (left) lays its eggs in fire ants' heads. This fire ant (right) died after a phorid-fly larva became a pupa.

Phorid flies

One of the biggest enemies of the fire ant is the phorid fly. It lays one egg at a time in a different fire ant's head. After a while, the egg hatches. The larva lives in the ant's head. When the fly larva enters its pupa stage, the fire ant's head falls off. The ant dies.

Leaf-cutter ants are nicknamed umbrella ants because the leaf pieces they carry look like umbrellas.

Leaf-cutter ants

Unlike army ants and fire ants, leaf-cutter ants do not eat meat or insects. Instead, they eat a special kind of fungus that grows only in their nests. A fungus is a plant-like living thing that feeds on rotting matter.

Leaf-cutter ants dig huge underground nests with many large chambers. The chambers are about 300 centimetres wide. They dig tunnels to connect the chambers together. They also dig special tunnels to let in air from outside.

Leaf-cutter ants use the chambers to grow the fungus that they eat. The ants are like farmers. They make sure there is enough heat and water for the fungus to grow.

Fungus gardens

A queen leaf-cutter ant starts a colony's fungus garden. She carries a piece of fungus with her when she leaves her old colony. She picks a new place and digs a small tunnel and chamber for herself. She places the piece of fungus in the chamber and puts special juices on the fungus to make it grow.

The queen then lays eggs. Once the eggs have turned into adult ants, some of the new workers dig more rooms and tunnels in the nest. Other workers leave the nest to find leaves. They use their mandibles to cut circles from the leaves. Then they carry these leaf pieces back to the nest.

The ants prepare the leaves. They lick the leaves to clean them. At night, the ants place leaves that are too dry outside to get wet. During the day, the ants put leaves that are too wet in the sun to dry.

Leaf-cutter ants begin chewing the leaves when they are just right for growing fungus. They spit out the chewed leaves and put them in the chambers. The fungus grows on the chewed, rotting leaves.

These leaf pieces will become food for the fungus.

Destroying the rainforest

The rainforest is home to thousands of other kinds of ants as well as army ants, fire ants and leaf-cutter ants. In some places, people are tearing down the rainforest to log, to farm, to raise cattle or to build homes. Ant colonies can only continue to live in the rainforest if people do not destroy it.

Glossary

abdomen (AB-duh-muhn) back section of an insect's body

Amazonia (am-uh-ZONE-ee-uh) largest rainforest in the world

antenna (an-TEN-uh) (plural **antennae**) body part on the head of some insects that allows them to touch, taste and smell objects around them

brood group of young; *also* the eggs, larvae and pupae of an ant colony

colony large group of living things that live and work together

fungus plant-like living thing that feeds on rotting matter

mandibles (MAN-di-buhls) mouthparts of the jaw that are used for biting and gripping

prey animals that are hunted by other animals for food

thorax (THOR-aks) middle part of an insect's body between its head and abdomen

venom poison produced by snakes, spiders and some insects

More information

Internet sites

Animals of the Rainforest
www.animalsoftherainforest.org

Rainforest Concern
www.rainforestconcern.org

Useful address

The Amateur Entomologists' Society Bug Club
PO Box 8774
London SW7 5ZG

Books to read

Macro, C; Hartley, K. *Bug Books: Ant*. Heinemann
　　Library, Oxford, 1999

Spilsbury, Louise and Richard. *Animal Groups:
　　Life in a Colony of Ants*. Heinemann Library,
　　Oxford, 2003

Index